Lord Byron: The Life and Legacy of the Most Famous Romantic Poet

By Charles River Editors

About Charles River Editors

Charles River Editors provides superior editing and original writing services across the digital publishing industry, with the expertise to create digital content for publishers across a vast range of subject matter. In addition to providing original digital content for third party publishers, we also republish civilization's greatest literary works, bringing them to new generations of readers via ebooks.

Sign up here to receive updates about free books as we publish them, and visit Our Kindle Author Page to browse today's free promotions and our most recently published Kindle titles.

Introduction

Lord Byron

"I am such a strange mélange of good and evil that it would be difficult to describe me." – Lord Byron

"Mad, bad, and dangerous to know." – Lady Caroline Lamb's description of Lord Byron

Lord Byron's very name conjures up visions of the Romantic movement and outlandishly dressed bohemians, for if Alfred, Lord Tennyson was the poetic darling of the masses, Byron was the hero of the hedonists. While the traditional English literary hero was a nobleman rescuing a damsel in distress, Byron created the anti-hero, a man plagued by self-doubt and hidden sorrow. At the same time, his hero was also capable of facing reality once he had wrestled through his own angst, and even of occasionally acting nobly in the great tradition of the author's Puritan forebears.

Whereas poets like Wordsworth and Browning were easy to love, Lord Byron inspired a certain amount of fear among the upper classes, and pious mothers were reluctant to let their daughters read his work. In a manner more appropriate to the 21st century than the 19th, Lord Byron was a man true to his own beliefs, supporting the rights of the oppressed even while enjoying all the benefits offered to him as a member of the British aristocracy.

If Byron himself was eclectic in his tastes and character, his poetry was even more so, for he could feature satiric pieces poking fun at the status quo and historical renditions of ancient battles fought with nobility and valor, all in the same volume. Like so many other writers, he used poetry to explore his own most deeply guarded secrets, in one poem playing in first person the dramatic hero and in another the troubled penitent. He was sometimes funny, sometimes lyrical, and sometimes verbose, but he was always interesting, and that is what allowed him to become one of the most famous writers of all time, almost against his own will, and despite his premature death.

Lord Byron: The Life and Legacy of the Most Famous Romantic Poet chronicles the life and work that made Lord Byron one of history's most famous poets. Along with pictures of important people, places, and events, you will learn about Lord Byron like never before.

Lord Byron: The Life and Legacy of the Most Famous Romantic Poet
About Charles River Editors
Introduction
   Byron's Childhood
   A Budding Writer
   The Grand Tour
   Back Home
   A Rendezvous with Destiny
   Online Resources
   Further Reading
Free Books by Charles River Editors
Discounted Books by Charles River Editors

Byron's Childhood

"Adversity is the first path to truth." – Lord Byron

George Gordon Noel Byron was born on January 22, 1788, in London, England. The midwife who delivered him was likely the first person to spot the imperfection that would shape the future poet's life, and perhaps even wrapped the baby up tightly so his mother, the former Catherine Gordon, might have a few moments with her newborn son before she, too, discovered there was something wrong with the baby's foot. Indeed, his right foot was clubbed, turning in at a right angle so that he would be forced all his life to walk on its outer side. This was yet another in a series of sorrows for young Catherine, whose husband, Captain John Byron, known to many as "Mad Jack," had already spent his own fortune and hers and was nowhere to be found when young George was born. Instead, Catherine had to face her son's problems with only her servants and 5 year old Augusta, Captain Byron's daughter from his first marriage, for comfort. Byron would later tell people that Mad Jack died by slitting his own throat, which wasn't true but was certainly indicative of what he thought of his absent father.

Mad Jack Byron

Catherine Gordon

Aware that she was now on her own, Catherine sent Augusta to live with her mother's family. A few months later, in 1789, she moved with her baby boy back to Aberdeen, where her parents were able to help shelter and provide for them. By this time, Mad Jack had fled to France in order to avoid his justifiably angry creditors. While there, he fell ill and died in 1791 at the age of 35 or 36, leaving his wife an emotionally unstable widow who focused all her energy on her son.

Unfortunately, Catherine's attention was far from consistently salutary, as she alternated between smothering the child with kisses and berating him for his inability to walk properly, depending on her mood. On the occasions when she did seek medical help for young George, she could very well fly into a rage if a doctor told her there was nothing they could do.

The one consistent presence in young George's life was his nurse, a strict Presbyterian who considered it her mission in life to train the young man in the ways of Calvinism and teach him as many Bible verses and stories as his young mind could hold. She also taught him to love the written word, which went a long way in ensuring that reading became his favorite pastime. Needless to say, she was instrumental in shaping his literary future, and she helped prepare him for a formal education at a young age. Byron later recalled, "I was sent, at five years old, or earlier, to a school kept by a Mr. Bowers, who was called 'Bodsy Bowers,' by reason of his dapperness. It was a school for both sexes. I learned little there except to repeat by rote the first lesson of monosyllables ('God made man' - 'Let us love him'), by hearing it often repeated, without acquiring a letter. Whenever proof was made of my progress, at home, I repeated these words with the most rapid fluency; but on turning over a new leaf, I continued to repeat them, so that the narrow boundaries of my first year's accomplishments were detected, my ears boxed, (which they did not deserve, seeing it was by ear only that I had acquired my letters,) and my intellects consigned to a new preceptor."

This new teacher proved to be quite an improvement, as Byron himself noted. "He was a very devout, clever, little clergyman, named Ross, afterwards minister of one of the kirks (East, I think). Under him I made astonishing progress; and I recollect to this day his mild manners and good-natured pains-taking. The moment I could read, my grand passion was history, and…I was particularly taken with the battle near the Lake Regillus in the Roman History, put into my hands the first…Afterwards I had a very serious, saturnine, but kind young man, named Paterson, for a tutor. … With him I began Latin in…and continued till I went to the 'Grammar School,'…where I threaded all the classes to the fourth, when I was recalled to England…. I acquired this handwriting, which I can hardly read myself, under the fair copies of Mr. Duncan of the same city: I don't think he would plume himself much upon my progress. However, I wrote much better then than I have ever done since. Haste and agitation of one kind or another have quite spoilt as pretty a scrawl as ever scratched over a frank."

In 1798, upon the death of his great-uncle, George returned to England to accept his new title as the sixth Baron Byron of Rochdale, and heir to Newstead Abbey in Nottinghamshire. He quickly embraced his new place in society and began his lifelong interest in all things associated with nobility.

Jim F. Bleak's picture of Byron's house in Nottinghamshire

As is often the case with young poets, Byron's first loves inspired him to make his first attempts at writing poetry. When he was just 8, he found himself attracted to one of his cousins, Mary Duff, of whom he wrote, "My mother used always to rally me about this childish amour, and at last, many years after, when I was sixteen, she told me one day, 'O Byron, I have had a letter from Edinburgh, and your old sweetheart, Mary Duff, is married to Mr. C***.' And what was my answer? I really cannot explain or account for my feelings at that moment, but they nearly threw me into convulsions...How the deuce did all this occur so early? Where could it originate? I certainly had no sexual ideas for years afterwards; and yet my misery, my love for that girl were so violent, that I sometimes doubt if I have ever been really attached since. Be that as it may, hearing of her marriage several years after was like a thunder-stroke – it nearly choked me – to the horror of my mother and the astonishment and almost incredulity of every body. And it is a phenomenon in my existence (for I was not eight years old) which has puzzled, and will puzzle me to the latest hour of it; and lately, I know not why, the recollection (not the attachment) has recurred as forcibly as ever...But, the more I reflect, the more I am bewildered to assign any cause for this precocity of affection… My passions were developed very early – so early, that few would believe me – if I were to state the period – and the facts which accompanied it. Perhaps this was one of the reasons that caused the anticipated melancholy of my thoughts – having anticipated life."

He wrote of another distant cousin, Margaret Parker, "It was the ebullition of passion for my first cousin, one of the most beautiful of evanescent beings I have long forgotten the verses, but it would be difficult for me to forget her - her dark eyes - her long eye-lashes, her completely Greek cast of face and figure! I was then about twelve - she rather older, perhaps a year. ... I do not recollect anything equal to the transparent beauty of my cousin, or to the sweetness of her temper, during the short period of our intimacy. She looked as if she had been made out of a rainbow, all beauty and peace."

Upon their return to England, Catherine enrolled her son in Harrow, one of the top schools in the nation. He developed his writing skills, while still finding time to engage in sports where, clad in a specially made boot, he was able to experience the joy that came from games with his peers. One of them later recalled, "Though he was lame, he was a great lover of sports, and preferred hockey to Horace, relinquished even Helig for 'duck puddle,' and gave up the best poet that ever wrote hard Latin for a game of cricket on the common. He was not remarkable (nor was he ever for his learning, but he was always a clever, plain spoken, and undaunted boy. I have seen him fight by the hour like a Trojan, and stand up against disadvantage of his lameness with all the spirit of an ancient combatant."

A Budding Writer

"We are all selfish and I no more trust myself than others with a good motive." – Lord Byron

Young love once again interrupted Byron's life in 1803, when he became enamored with his cousin, Mary Chaworth, who was already engaged to someone else. He later raved, "She was the beau ideal of all that my youthful fancy could paint of beautiful and I have taken all my fables about the celestial nature of women from the perfection my imagination created in her. I say created, for I found her, like the rest of the sex, anything but angelic. ... I now began to fancy myself a man, and to make love in earnest." Unfortunately for the young teen, even he had to admit that "the ardour was all on my side; I was serious, she was volatile. She liked me as a younger brother, and treated and laughed at me as a boy; she, however, gave me her picture, and that was something to make verses upon. Had I married Miss Chaworth, perhaps the whole tenour of my life would have been different…"

Indeed, it was to Mary Chaworth that he penned "Hills of Annesley" in 1805, just after she married her betrothed:

> "Hills of Annesley, bleak and barren,
>
> Where my thoughtless childhood stray'd,

How the northern tempests, warring,

Howl above thy tufted shade!

Now no more, the hours beguiling,

Former favourite haunts I see;

Now no more my Mary smiling

Makes ye seem a heaven to me."

By this time, Byron had yet another woman in his life. He had reached out to his half-sister, Augusta, and initiated a relationship with her that would provide a healthy antidote to his mother's ongoing madness. He also enrolled in Trinity College at Cambridge, though this did not please him. He explained, "Firstly, I so much disliked leaving Harrow. Secondly, I wished to go to Oxford, and not to Cambridge. Thirdly, I was so completely alone in this new world, that it half broke my spirits. It was one of the deadliest and heaviest feelings of my life to feel that I was no longer a boy." Perhaps this is why he developed a number of bad habits that would plague him throughout his life while at Cambridge, including gambling and living beyond his means.

Augusta

Fortunately, Byron continued writing, and by the end of 1806 he had published his first book of poetry, *Fugitive Pieces*. Most notably, by paying for the work himself, Byron was able to include certain passages that would not have gotten past most early 19th century publishers. When his spiritual and literary mentor, the local minister John Becher, complained about the erotic nature of some of the poems, Byron responded immediately by withdrawing the volume from distribution. He edited the offensive poems and released it again in early 1807 under the title *Poems on Various Occasions.* Too fearful of the outcome of his short life's work to place his name on either volume, he waited until the books were well received before publishing a third version, *Hours of Idleness*, under the name of "George Gordon, Lord Byron, A Minor."

He need not have included that last comment, for anyone reading "On A Change Of Masters At A Great Public School" would have realized that a very young man wrote it, given that he seemed compelled to squeeze in as many references to his classical education as possible:

> "Where are those honours, Ida! once your own,
> When Probus fill'd your magisterial throne?
> As ancient Rome, fast falling to disgrace,

Hail'd a Barbarian in her Cæsar's place,
So you, degenerate, share as hard a fate,
And seat Pomposus where your Probus sate.
Of narrow brain, yet of a narrower soul,
Pomposus holds you in his harsh controul;
Pomposus, by no social virtue sway'd,
With florid jargon, and with vain parade;
With noisy nonsense, and new-fangled rules,
(Such as were ne'er before enforc'd in schools.)
Mistaking pedantry for learning's laws,
He governs, sanction'd but by self-applause;
With him the same dire fate, attending Rome,
Ill-fated Ida! soon must stamp your doom;
Like her o'erthrown, for ever lost to fame,
No trace of science left you, but the name."

The volume would go one to enjoy a second edition, this time as *Poems Original and Translated,* in 1808. By that point, Byron had resumed his education at Cambridge and had joined his new friend, John Cam Hobhouse, in the Cambridge Whig Club.

Hobhouse

In its January 1808 edition, the *Edinburgh Review* published a scathing review of *Hours of*

Idleness. Written by Henry Brougham, it challenged Byron on both a professional and a personal level: "The poesy of this young lord belongs to the class which neither gods nor men are said to permit. Indeed, we do not recollect to have seen a quantity of verse with so few deviations in either direction from that exact standard. His effusions are spread over a dead flat, and can no more get above or below the level, than if they were so much stagnant water. As an extenuation of this offence, the noble author is peculiarly forward in pleading minority. We have it in the title-page, and on the very back of the volume; it follows his name like a favourite part of his style. Much stress is laid upon it in the preface, and the poems are connected with this general statement of his case, by particular dates, substantiating the age at which each was written…Now, the law upon the point of minority, we hold to be perfectly clear. It is a plea available only to the defendant; no plaintiff can offer it as a supplementary ground of action. Thus, if any suit could be brought against Lord Byron, for the purpose of compelling him to put into court a certain quantity of poetry; and if judgement were given against him; it is highly probable that an exception would be taken, were he to deliver for poetry, the contents of this volume…whatever judgment may be passed on the poems of this noble minor, it seems we must take them as we find them, and be content; for they are the last we shall ever have from him. He is at best, he says, but an intruder into the groves of Parnassus; he never lived in a garret, like thorough-bred poets; and 'though he once roved a careless mountaineer in the Highlands of Scotland,' he has not of late enjoyed this advantage. Moreover, he expects no profit from his publication; and whether it succeeds or not, 'it is highly improbable, from his situation and pursuits hereafter,' that he should again condescend to become an author. Therefore, let us take what we get and be thankful. What right have we poor devils to be nice?"

Brougham

Fortunately for his readers and posterity, Byron responded powerfully to the criticism and shifted his attention to writing satire. In the spring of 1809, he published *English Bards, and Scotch Reviewers, A Satire*. In the preface of this work, Byron proclaimed, "All my friends, learned and unlearned, have urged me not to publish this Satire with my name. If I were to be 'turned from the career of my humour by quibbles quick, and papers bullets of the brain,' I should have complied with their counsel. But I am not...terrified by abuse, or bullied by reviewers, with or without arms. I can safely say that I have attacked none personally, who did not commence on the offensive. An author's works are public property: he who purchases may judge, and publish his opinion if he pleases; and the authors I have endeavoured to commemorate may do by me as I have done by them. I dare say they will succeed better in condemning my scribblings, than in mending their own. But my object is not to prove that I can write well, but if possible, to make other write better...With regard to the real talents of many of the poetical persons whose performances are mentioned or alluded to in the following pages, it is presumed by the author that there can be little difference in opinion in the public at large; though, like other sectaries, each has his separate tabernacle of proselytes, by whom his abilities are over-rated, his faults overlooked, and his metrical canons received without scruple and without consideration...But the unquestionable possession of considerable genius by several of the writers here censured renders their mental prostitution more to be regretted. Imbecility may be pitied, or, at worst, laughed at and forgotten: perverted powers demand the most decided reprehension. No one can wish more than the author that some known and able writer had undertaken their exposure; but Mr. Giffford has devoted himself to Massinger, and, in the absence of the regular physician, a country practitioner may, in cases of absolute necessity, be allowed to prescribe his nostrum to prevent the extension of so deplorable an epidemic, provided there be no quackery in his treatment of the malady. A caustic is here offered; as it is to be feared nothing short of actual cautery can recover the Edinburgh Reviewers, it would indeed require an Hercules to crush the Hydra; but if the author succeeds in merely 'bruising one of the heads of the serpent,' though his own hand should suffer in the encounter, he will be amply satisfied."

Byron then presented his readers with a collection of poetry devoted to skewering many of the poets and playwrights of his day, from Walter Scott to Richard Brinsley Sheridan. However, he saved his most vicious attacks for those who would criticize the work of others, taking special aim at Francis Jeffrey, who he initially thought wrote the nasty comments about him in the *Edinburgh Review*.

Jeffrey

RICHARD BRINSLEY SHERIDAN
From a crayon drawing by John Russell

Sheridan

Byron soon realized that he had found his true voice in satire, and the critics, even some of the ones he lambasted, agreed. In March 1809, *The Gentleman's Magazine* said, "The Poem before us is unquestionably the result of an impassioned yet diligent study of the best masters, grounded on a fine taste and very happy natural endowments. It unites much of the judgment of the Essay on Criticism, the playful yet poignant smile and frown of indignation and ridicule of the Dunciad, with the versification of the Epistle to Arbuthnot, and the acuteness of the Imitations of Horace of the same Author; at the same time that we think we have discovered a resemblance of the best epigrammatic points and brilliant turns of the Love of Fame. And with all this it is unquestionably an original work. In a word, many years have passed since the English press has given us a performance so replete with mingled genius, good sense, and spirited animadversion."

The Gentleman's Magazine obviously knew what it was talking about, for the poem's popularity quickly spread, and within a few months Byron had a second, expanded edition printed. He had also claimed authorship of it, a decision he soon had reason to regret, because that June, *The Cabinet* seemed to challenge his authorship. "Satire seems the order of the day. It is reported that this little volume is the vengeful retort of Lord Byron on the severity of the Edinburgh Review, in their critique of his Poems; but, besides that we think the Satire is written with more talent than Lord Byron possesses, many more persons than Scotch Reviewers, and even than English Bards, come under the present lash." Obviously, part of the problem lay in the fact that many of those writing the reviews were themselves victims of Byron's barbs, as William Gifford noted when he wrote to Francis Hodgson on June 3, "Lord Byron's poem sells well I understand. I have an angry review of it, which I shall not use; for though it is well written, it is manifestly unjust. Unless works can be made to amuse or instruct the reader, it is loss of time to dwell long on them or indeed to mention them at all." For 1808-1809, the *Poetical Register* added, "The luckless wights who have brought upon themselves the hostility of Lord Byron have ample cause to regret their rashness. He wields the scourge of satire with a vigorous and unrelenting hand. We do not recollect that anything half so severe as this poem has appeared since the days of the Baviad and the Maeviad. Though in some instances we must dissent from the judgment passed by his Lordship, we think that the censure which he bestows is generally well merited by the objects of it, and that he has done a considerable service to the cause of justice and of good taste."

Byron would go on to release two more editions of the poem in 1810, but they would be the last published under his hand, for he learned in time to respect many of those he had criticized, and thus chose not to publish any further versions.

The Grand Tour

"Why I came here, I know not; where I shall go it is useless to inquire - in the midst of myriads of the living and the dead worlds, stars, systems, infinity, why should I be anxious about an atom?" – Lord Byron

While Byron might have been better served using some of the money he made to pay off his mounting debts, he instead boarded a ship bound for Lisbon on July 2, 1809. From there, he and his traveling companions, including Hobhouse, William Fletcher (his valet), Robert Rushton (of *Childe Harold's Pilgrimage* fame) and another servant, proceeded across Spain on horseback to Greece, following the path the Duke of Wellington had recently taken during the Peninsular Campaign against Napoleon's French Empire. According to Byron scholar Peter Cochran, "When they were at Malta in September 1809, Byron and his friend Hobhouse took eleven lessons in Arabic, probably from the Abbate Giacchino Navarro, Librarian at the Valletta Public Library. This seems a sure sign they had arrived with no firm intention of going either to Greece or to Constantinople, for in neither place would Arabic be of any use…on the 3rd, however, they met a man who, seeing two young, impressionable and directionless Englishmen, one of whom was of striking beauty, decided to charm them into his circle, and to send them to Albania, to Ali Pasha. The man was Spiridion Foresti, sometime English Consul on Corfu, but now out of a job."

It was in Ioannina that Byron purchased the Eastern clothing in which he was later famously painted. He also met Ali Pasha and his son, both of whom proved to be charming hosts and the inspiration for "*Don Juan*'s Lambro."

An 1813 painting of Byron

Filled with wonder at all he was experiencing, Byron began composing a lengthy poem detailing his adventures. It began in October 1809 as a tale of Childe Buron (Child Byron), but he later renamed his character Harold, perhaps feeling that he was not quite prepared to be that open with his audience. He completed the first canto of the poem during Christmas that year.

By the end of 1809, Byron was staying in Athens with a Greek widow named Tarsia Macri,\ and her daughters. He recorded in his diary, "[W]e occupied two houses separated from each other only by a single wall through which opened a doorway. One of them belongs to a Greek lady, whose name is Theodora (sic) Macri…and who has to show many letters of recommendation, left in her hands by several English travelers. Her lodgings consisted of a sitting-room and two bedrooms, opening into a court-yard where there were five or six lemon trees, from which, during our residence in the place, was plucked the fruit that seasoned the pilaf, and other national dishes served up at our frugal table."

In 2016, *The National Herald* observed, "The poem, 'Maid of Athens,' was written when Byron was leaving Athens in 1810, and it was dedicated to Teresa Makri. In a letter to H. Drury, May 3, 1810, Byron wrote: 'I almost forgot to tell you that I am dying for the love of three Greek Girls at Athens, sisters, two of whom have promised to accompany me to England, I lived in the same house, Teresa, Mariana, and Kattinka, are the names of these divinities all of them under 15…' What Byron leaves out of his letter to Drury, is an event that may or may not have taken place. After Byron's return to England, a story soon circulated. First credited to Byron confidant Thomas Moore, this story contends that Byron had so loved Teresa Makri that he 'was on his knees before her with a dagger pointed at his bare chest entreating her to take him or kill him!'"

Teresa as an old woman in 1870

The question of who the "Maid of Athens" was has plagued scholars for decades. Some claim that it was one of Makri's daughters, while others believe it was Makri herself. It could even be some other woman that he met in Greece. Regardless, "Maid of Athens" remains one of Byron's most beloved poems:

> "Maid of Athens, ere we part,
>
> Give, oh give me back my heart!
>
> Or, since that has left my breast,
>
> Keep it now, and take the rest!
>
> Hear my vow before I go,
>
> "Ζώη μου σάς άγαπώ"
>
> By those tresses unconfined,
>
> Woo'd by each Aegean wind;
>
> By those lids whose jetty fringe
>
> Kiss thy soft cheeks blooming tinge;
>
> By those wild eyes like the roe,
>
> "Ζώη μου σάς άγαπώ"
>
> By that lip I long to taste;
>
> By that zone-encircled waist;
>
> By all the token-flowers that tell
>
> What words can never speak so well;
>
> By love's alternate joy and woe,
>
> "Ζώη μου σάς άγαπώ"
>
> Maid of Athens! I am gone:
>
> Think of me, sweet! when alone.
>
> Though I fly to Istambol,

Athens holds my heart and soul:

Can I cease to love thee? No!

"Ζώη μου σάς άγαπώ"

  For all the passion contained in those words, those who have studied Byron's life remain unsure whether they are evidence of romantic feelings towards a girl. For example, Christopher Brouzas noted, "Writers disagree on the intensity or sincerity of Byron's affection towards Teresa, some thinking that he was really in love, while others maintain that it was a mild case of romance…If we were to take him literally, we might argue that he was really in love, if only for a short time. But whatever Byron's real affections may have been…when he wrote his farewell to the Maid of Athens…they certainly cooled off rather rapidly."

  As Byron fell in love with the people of Greece and Albania, both individually and collectively, he also began to grieve for what was happening to their culture. He had already criticized the Earl of Elgin, Thomas Bruce, for his part in looting "Mis-shapen monuments and maimed antiques" from Greece, and now that he saw the ruins with his own eyes, he became even more indignant. Writing for Oxford University Press in 1983, William St. Clair explained, "When Byron came to Greece, one afternoon, he went as a pilgrim to visit the Acropolis of Athens but was shocked at the plight of the Parthenon, the temple of goddess of wisdom Minerva. The sacrilege Lord Elgin had committed was still fresh. Byron, an admirer of the beauty of the ancient Greek sculpture, felt ashamed for what his compatriot Elgin did only 10 years earlier. Such was Byron's indignation that he composed his most severe satire attacking Elgin's odious crime, 'The Curse of Minerva.'"

Lord Elgin

"The Curse of Minerva" begins with a moving description of Byron's feelings as he watched the sun set behind the Acropolis:

> "Slow sinks, more lovely ere his race be run,
>
> Along Morea's hills the setting sun;
>
> Not, as in northern climes, obscurely bright,
>
> But one unclouded blaze of living light;
>
> O'er the hushed deep the yellow beam he throws,
>
> Gilds the green wave that trembles as it glows;
>
> On old Aegina's rock and Hydra's isle the god of gladness sheds his parting smile;
>
> O'er his own regions lingering loves to shine,
>
> Though there his altars are no more divine.

> Descending fast, the mountain-shadows kiss
>
> Thy glorious Gulf, unconquered Salamis!
>
> Their azure arches through the long expanse,
>
> More deeply purpled, meet his mellowing glance,
>
> And tenderest tints, along their summits driven,
>
> Mark his gay course, and own the hues of Heaven;
>
> Till, darkly shaded from the land and deep
>
> Behind his Delphian rock he sinks to sleep."

Byron editor Peter Cochran later noted, "Byron uses Elgin's supposed larceny (the firman allowing him to take the marbles was legal), as a parallel to such disparate crises as the attack on Copenhagen; an army mutiny in India; the victory by starving English soldiers over the French at Barossa in Spain; and incipient famine and disorder at home – things in which imperialist cultural expropriation figures only remotely. Is the guilt Britannia should feel for them the same as she should feel about Elgin's despoliation of the Parthenon, or are they a consequence of Minerva's anger at the despoliation? Logic is not the poem's strong point, and we search for an answer with difficulty. It looks as though Elgin's model for his crime is the behaviour of his burglarious motherland – even though the problems of the Baltic, India, and Spain, are English, not Scots, as in consistency they should be."

On March 19, 1810, Byron wrote to his mother, "I have traversed the greatest part of Greece, besides Epirus, &c. &c., resided ten weeks at Athens, and am now on the Asiatic side on my way to Constantinople. I have just returned from viewing the ruins of Ephesus, a day's journey from Smyrna. I presume you have received a long letter I wrote from Albania, with an account of my reception by the Pacha of the province. When I arrive at Constantinople, I shall determine whether to proceed into Persia or return, which latter I do not wish, if I can avoid it…I shall stand in need of remittances whether I proceed or return. I have written to him repeatedly, that he may not plead ignorance of my situation for neglect. I can give you no account of anything, for I have not time or opportunity, the frigate sailing immediately. … Greece, particularly in the vicinity of Athens, is delightful, — cloudless skies and lovely landscapes."

As he stayed on the move, Byron completed Canto II of *Childe Harold* on March 28, 1810. By this time, he and Hobhouse had reached Turkey, where they visited the supposed site of Troy and swam the Hellespont, as Leander had in Ovid's *Hero and Leander*. However, Byron soon became disenchanted with Turkey and returned to Athens, where he lodged in a Capuchin monastery and studied Italian and Greek with the monks for a number of months. He focused much of his time on writing, composing notes on *Childe Harold* to explain some of its more obscure points to his audience.

He also composed two poems in the early spring of 1811. The first was "Hints from Horace," something of a sequel to "English Bards, and Scotch Reviewers," in which he turned his satiric wit on the poets and dramatists of his age. However, he did not publish it, writing to Francis Hodgson in October 1811that "the Hints from Horace (to which I have subjoined some savage lines on Methodism, and ferocious notes on the vanity of the triple Editory of the Edin. Annual Register), my Hints, I say, stand still, and why? — I have not a true friend in the world (but you and Drury) who can construe Horace's Latin or my English well enough to adjust them for the press, or to correct the proofs in a grammatical way." It would later be published after his death. The second poem was "The Curse of Minerva," mentioned earlier.

Back Home

"I only know we loved in vain;

I only feel — farewell! farewell!" – Lord Byron

Byron returned to England in April 1811, arriving in Kent on July 14 with enough life experiences to produce a large body of work. In fact, he would start producing it in the years that followed, but before then, he would suffer immense grief, for on August 2, his beloved mother died. Heartbroken, he wrote, "I had but one friend in the world and she is gone." He would later complain that his mother "was as haughty as Lucifer, with her descent from the Stuarts and her line from the old Gordons—not the Seyton Gordons, as she disdainfully termed the ducal branch. She told me the story, always reminding me how superior Gordons were to the southern Byrons, notwithstanding our Norman and always masculine descent." While the statements seem contradictory, he no doubt meant both at different times.

More grief followed when he learned of the death of another close friend, John Edleston, for whom Byron might have harbored romantic feelings. In 1811, he wrote the first of several "To Thyrza" poems in his honor, writing under the guise of the subject's feminine name:

> "By many a shore and many a sea
>
> Divided, yet beloved in vain;
>
> The Past, the Future fled to thee,
>
> To bid us meet --- no --- ne'er again !
>
>
> Could this have been --- a word, a look,

That softly said, 'We part in peace,'

Had taught my bosom how to brook,

With fainter sighs, thy soul's release.

And didst thou not, since Death for thee

Prepared a light and pangless dart,

Once long for him thou ne'er shall see

Who held, and holds thee in his heart?

Oh ! Who like him had watch'd thee here?

Or sadly mark'd thy glazing eye,

In that dread hour ere death appear,

When silent sorrow fears to sigh,"

After a number of stanzas that might have been written about a dear but platonic friend, Byron became more specific:

"Ours too the glance none saw beside;

The smile none else might understand;

The whisper'd thought of hearts allied,

The pressure of the thrilling hand.

The kiss, so guiltless and refined,

That Love each warmer wish forbore;

Those eyes proclaim'd so pure a mind

Even Passion blush'd to plead for more.

> The tone, that taught me to rejoice,
>
> When prone, unlike thee, to repine;
>
> The song, celestial from thy voice,
>
> But sweet to me from none but thine;"

Byron also alluded to some piece of jewelry or other gift that the two men shared as a token of their feelings for each other:

> "The pledge we wore --- I wear it still,
>
> But where is thine? --- Ah ! Where art thou?
>
> Oft have I borne the weight of ill,
>
> But never bent beneath till now !
>
> Well hast thou left in life's best bloom
>
> The cup of woe for me to drain.
>
> If rest alone be in the tomb,
>
> I would not wish thee here again."

After months of mourning, Byron rejoined public life in January 1812 when he returned to the House of Lords. There, on February 27, he made the first of only three political speeches he would give during his life. Speaking on behalf of stocking weavers in Nottinghamshire who had broken the machinery brought in to replace them, he said, "The perseverance of these miserable men in their proceedings, tends to prove that nothing but absolute want could have driven a large and once honest and industrious body of the people into the commission of excesses so hazardous to themselves, their families, and the community. At the time to which I allude, the town and county were burdened with large detachments of the military; the police was in motion, the magistrates assembled, yet all these movements, civil and military had led to—nothing. Not a single instance had occurred of the apprehension of any real delinquent actually taken in the fact, against whom there existed legal evidence sufficient for conviction."

Byron went on to admit, "Considerable injury has been done to the proprietors of the improved frames. These machines were to them an advantage, inasmuch as they superseded the necessity of employing a number of workmen, who were left in consequence to starve. By the adoption of one species of frame in particular, one man performed the work of many, and the superfluous labourers were thrown out of employment." At the same time, Byron insisted that "the work thus executed was inferior in quality, not marketable at home, and merely hurried over with a view to exportation…These men never destroyed their looms till they were become useless, worse than useless; till they were become actual impediments to their exertions in obtaining their daily bread. Can you then wonder, that in times like these, when bankruptcy, convicted fraud, and imputed felony, are found in a station not far beneath that of your Lordships, the lowest, though once most useful portion of the people, should forget their duty in their distresses, and become only less guilty than one of their representatives ? But while the exalted offender can find means to baffle the law, new capital punishments must be devised, new snares of death must be spread, for the wretched mechanic who is famished into guilt. These men were willing to dig, but the spade was in other hands; they were not ashamed to beg, but there was none to relieve them. Their own means of subsistence were cut off; all other employments pre-occupied; and their excesses, however to be deplored and condemned, can hardly be the subject of surprise."

Following this speech, Byron confessed to a friend, "I spoke very violent sentences with a sort of modest impudence, abused everything and everybody, put the Lord Chancellor very much out of humour, and if I may believe what I hear, have not lost any character in the experiment".

The following month, John Murray II published *Child Harold's Pilgrimage*, which sold out in just three days. Byron spoke before the House of Lords on to two other occasions in the months that followed, but he quickly lost interest in politics and returned to poetry. Writing for the *Edinburgh Review*, Francis Jeffrey, who Byron had savaged, admitted, "LORD BYRON has improved marvellously since his last appear at our tribunal; — and this, though it bear a very affected title, is really a volume of very considerable power, spirit and originality — which not only atones for the evil works of his nonage, but gives promise of a further excellence hereafter; to which it is quite comfortable to look forward…The most surprising thing about the present work, indeed, is, that it should please and interest so much as it does, with so few of the ordinary ingredients of interest or poetical delight. … As there are no incidents, there cannot well be any characters; — and accordingly, with the exception of a few national sketches, which form part of the landscape of his pilgrimage, that of the hero himself is the only delineation of the kind that is offered to the reader of this volume; — and this hero, we must say, appears to us as oddly chosen as he is imperfectly employed. *Childe Harold* is a sated epicure — sickened with the very fulness of prosperity — oppressed with ennui, and stung with occasional remorse; — his heart hardened by sensual indulgence, and his opinion of mankind degraded by his acquaintance with the baser part of them. In this state he wanders over the fairest and most interesting parts of Europe, in the vain hope of stimulating his palsied sensibility by novelty; or at least of occasionally forgetting his mental anguish in the toils and perils of his journey."

At least one author considered Harold to be the first "Byronic Hero," and in 2009, author Ian Dennis observed in his book, *Lord Byron and the History of Desire*, "Some two thousand years later Byron is responding to…a changed situation, in which the relation to the sacred center is more intimate and, indeed, can be conceived of not just as rivalrous, but as reciprocal. … In short, this is the world of internal mediation, in which the nearby model, who is also an obstacle and can easily become a subject in his turn, must participate with his or her Other in a duel of desires, the goal of which is to make the Other the subjected imitator of his or her own desire...The desire that Byron's poem describes, and that is the virulent core of internal mediation, is, again, what René Girard called 'metaphysical' desire: imitative desire in which external objects of desire have dropped out of the triangular structure, leaving the two subject-models face to face. ...an absence of desire for external objects can only be interpreted, by rivals, as a secret and triumphantly gratified desire for oneself, and this apparent-because-hidden desire attracts imitation. That is, it has a particular power to subject others. (Less secret desire, obvious pride, however, turns back toward a kind of external object, an externalized self, and thus betrays a desire for the admiration of others. Pride goes before subjection, goes before a fall, into it.) Genuine power therefore lies with those who can most persuasively demonstrate indifference toward any and every external good, who can betray in any context less desire. Internal mediation in its intensest registers pits such demonstrations against each other, in contests increasingly stripped of every structurally guaranteed advantage: rank or person or any form of sacral difference. In such a situation even a sky god's desires will no longer automatically attract those of earth dwellers."

With this latest publication, Byron found himself the toast of London as aristocratic hostesses fought to get him to attend their parties, even giving some in his honor. Among these charming women dripping in diamonds was Lady Caroline Lamb, with whom he enjoyed a passionate but short lived affair during the summer of 1812. When the weather cooled, so did Byron's passions, though she remained smitten and took to all sorts of romantic theatrics, going so far as to purchase pictures of him just so she could burn them.

A painting of Lady Caroline

On the other hand, Lamb's mother-in-law, the unflappable Lady Melbourne, took the entire affair in stride and even arranged for Byron to propose to her niece, the bookish Annabella Milbanke. Byron wrote of her, "There was something piquant, and what we term pretty, in Miss Millbank; her features were small and feminine, though not regular; she had the fairest skin imaginable; her figure was perfect for her height, and there was a simplicity, a retired modesty about her, which was very characteristic, and formed a happy contrast to the cold artificial formality and studied stiffness which is called fashion: she interested me exceedingly…It is unnecessary to detail the progress of our acquaintance: I became daily more attached to her, and it ended in my making her a proposal that was rejected; her refusal was couched in terms that could not offend me."

Lady Melbourne

Annabella

As time passed, Lady Lamb decided to turn her longings into readable form by writing *Glenarvon*, based on their affair, or at least her version of it. Published in 1816, the book is considered by many to be the first novel to ever feature a vampire. While Glenarvon, the character patterned after Byron, drained the blood from his victims, he did not drink it, but he was unquestionably a sinister character. Lady Lamb wrote that Glenarvon "wandered forth every evening by the pale moon, and no one knew whither he went….And when the rain fell heavy and chill, he would bare his forehead to the storm; and faint and weary wander forth, and often he smiled on others and appeared calm, whilst the burning fever of his blood continued to rage within." In another place, she claimed, 'When he smiled it was like the light radiance of heaven; and when he spoke, his voice was more soothing in its sweetness than music…"

According to literary historian David Ellis, "One of Byron's weaknesses, to which most of his friends quickly accommodated themselves, was that he would casually show the letters he received to third parties. It is a major complaint of Calantha against Glenarvon that he does so with hers. Lamb was also furious to discover that her own letters had been read by others and she retaliated by giving to phrases he had both written and said to her the wider currency of a novel. They were a reminder, highly uncomfortable to Byron if not to a wider public, of how infatuated he had once been with Caroline Lamb. … Glenarvon dies too but only at the very end of the novel and after being loaded with crimes, including the abduction of one small child and the murder of another."

By the time *Glenarvon* came out, Byron had achieved a level of notoriety that protected him from any negative fallout from his association with the novel. By then, he had published six very popular works from 1813-1816, most of them centered around his travels. The first, *The Giaou*, was published in June 1813, and Waafa Kada noted of it, "Byron's poem The Giaour subtitled 'A Fragment of a Turkish Tale' is a disjointed fragment of an Oriental tale. ... The poem deviates from any of Byron's poems by remaining the only one ever revised after the initial drafting. The first version constituted 375 lines and it has been, in Byron's words, 'lengthening its rattles' until the seventh edition when it reached its final length of 1,334 lines. According to one of Byron's letters, 'the circumstances to which the above story relates are not very uncommon in Turkey.' He overheard it 'by accident recited in one of the coffee-house storytellers who abound in the Levant.' However, regarding the fragmented style, he put the blame on a 'failure of memory.' The poem suggests a story at the level of a narrative which juxtaposes the Eastern and Western concepts of love, life and the afterlife, as well as a binary opposition between East and West, Islam and Christianity."

A few months after he released *The Giaour*, Byron published *The Bride of Abydos* in December. Of this latest attempt, he wrote to Moore, "All convulsions end with me in rhyme; and to solace my midnights, I have scribbled another Turkish Tale." In this book, he discussed the taboo subject of incest, a topic he was particularly interested in because, during this period, Byron had formed the most unusual relationship of his life, a romantic entanglement with his half-sister Augusta. Augusta was 30 years old, five years older than Byron, and was married to Colonel George Leigh, her own cousin, with whom she had three children. As biographer Will Durant pointed out, "she was affectionate, accommodating, perhaps a bit awed by her brother's fame, and inclined to give him whatever she could command. Her long separation from him, added to her husband's neglect, left her emotionally free. Byron, who had rashly discarded any moral taboo that had not met the test of his young reason, wondered why he should not mate with his sister, as the Pharaohs had done...Later developments indicate that he now, or soon, had sexual relations with Augusta. In August of this year 1813 he thought of taking her with him on a Mediterranean voyage. That plan fell through, but in January he took her to Newstead Abbey. When, on April 15, 1814, Augusta gave birth to a daughter, Byron wrote to Lady Melbourne that 'if it is an ape, that must be my fault'; the child herself, Medora Leigh, came to believe herself his daughter. In May he sent Augusta three thousand pounds to clear her husband's debts. In July he was with her in Hastings. In August he took her to his Abbey."

By that point, Byron had published *The Corsair* in February 1814. One of his most popular works, it would become the inspiration for the opera *Il corsaro* by Giuseppe Verdi, as well as a number of other musical pieces.

Byron also continued to pursue Milbanke, ultimately convincing her in late 1814 to accept his offer of marriage. It seems that Milbanke had at least some understanding of what she was getting herself into, as she wrote a friend in October, "It is not in the great world that Lord

Byron's true character must be sought; but ask of those nearest to him—of the unhappy whom he has consoled, of the poor whom he has blessed, of the dependents to whom he has been the best of masters. For his despondency I fear I am too answerable for the last two years. I have a calm and deep security—a confidence in God and man." Though he suffered from excessively cold feet, Byron ultimately married her on January 2, 1815, a few months after he completed *Lara*. Published in August 1814, it was something of a sequel to *The Corsair*, and like the others it sold well.

On April 10, 1814, Byron parted from his travelogue writings long enough to weigh in on the most pressing issue of the day. By then, Britons were hopeful that Napoleon, the French emperor, was doomed to be driven from his throne into exile, an idea that troubled Byron. His "Ode to Napoleon Buonaparte" is as ambivalent as its author's own feelings, for while he was attracted to Napoleon's heroic masculinity, he was appalled by the way the French had sacked and looted the countries they conquered.

In keeping with the ambivalence that plagued so many aspects of his life, Byron, at a time when he was embracing some of the most forbidden activities in Judeo-Christian tradition, began to work with Issac Nathan on a series of Hebrew Melodies that would be sung in Nathan's synagogue. The project held special appeal for Byron, who was a devoted reader of the Bible, even as he ignored so many of its teachings and was privately agnostic. Their work proved to be an excellent seller and contained one of his most famous poems:

> "She walks in beauty, like the night
> Of cloudless climes and starry skies;
> And all that's best of dark and bright
> Meet in her aspect and her eyes:
> Thus mellowed to that tender light
> Which heaven to gaudy day denies.
>
> One shade the more, one ray the less,
> Had half impaired the nameless grace
> Which waves in every raven tress,
> Or softly lightens o'er her face;
> Where thoughts serenely sweet express,
> How pure, how dear their dwelling-place.
>
> And on that cheek, and o'er that brow,
> So soft, so calm, yet eloquent,
> The smiles that win, the tints that glow,
> But tell of days in goodness spent,
> A mind at peace with all below,

A heart whose love is innocent!"

Upon marrying, the young couple moved to Piccadilly Terrace in London, but within months, the honeymoon was both literally and figuratively over. Byron, suffering from acute depression, likely inherited from his mother and brought on by his debts, began to abuse Annabella both mentally and physically. He also began cheating on her with actress Susan Boyce, even as Annabella was pregnant and concerned for her husband's sanity. When their only child, Ada, was born on December 10, 1815, Byron became even more despondent, and a month later, he sent Annabella and the baby home to live with her parents. Once safely out of his reach, Annabella began making a case for legal separation, which she obtained in March 1816, just a month after Byron published *The Siege of Corinth and Parisina,* his final tale of Eastern lore. Having rid himself of wife and child, Byron decided it was time to go abroad again, leaving April 25 for Ostend.

Ada as a child

Ada as an adult

He would never return.

A Rendezvous with Destiny

"There is pleasure in the pathless woods, there is rapture in the lonely shore, there is society where none intrudes, by the deep sea, and music in its roar; I love not Man the less, but Nature more." – Lord Byron

"If they had said that the sun or the moon had gone out of the heavens, it could not have struck me with the idea of a more awful and dreary blank in creation than the words: 'Byron is dead!'" - Jane Welsh Carlyle

Once he was abroad again, Byron would make his home among the glittering salons and damp castles of Europe, but if he thought that leaving England would free him from the consequences of his past dalliances, he was wrong. No sooner had he arrived in Geneva on May 25 than an obviously pregnant Claire Clairmont, with whom he had enjoyed a torrid affair some months earlier, showed up at his door. However, she seemed to show him no ill will; in fact, she brought with her Mary Shelley and Mary Godwin, setting the stage for one of the greatest literary friendships of all time. It was while staying in Geneva and telling ghost stories in front of the fire at night that Shelley wrote her most famous novel, *Frankenstein; or, The Modern Prometheus*, which was published in 1818.

Clairmont

Shelley

Byron also kept himself busy around this time by writing "The Prisoner of Chillon." It was based on the story of Francois Bonivard, who was kept for a time in the dungeon of the Chateau de Chillon, which Byron and Shelley visited in June 1816. The work vividly described what they saw there:

> "There are seven pillars of Gothic mould,
>
> In Chillon's dungeons deep and old,
>
> There are seven columns, massy and grey,
>
> Dim with a dull imprison'd ray,
>
> A sunbeam which hath lost its way,
>
> And through the crevice and the cleft
>
> Of the thick wall is fallen and left;

Creeping o'er the floor so damp,

Like a marsh's meteor lamp:

And in each pillar there is a ring,

And in each ring there is a chain;

That iron is a cankering thing,

For in these limbs its teeth remain,

With marks that will not wear away,

Till I have done with this new day,

Which now is painful to these eyes,

Which have not seen the sun so rise

For years—I cannot count them o'er,

I lost their long and heavy score

When my last brother droop'd and died,

And I lay living by his side."

The tale proved to be so popular that it nearly overshadowed the publication in late 1816 of the third canto of *Childe Harold*, which Byron declared to be his favorite poem.

In August 1816, Hobhouse joined Byron's party, just as the ladies were leaving. Claire was by this time well into her second trimester and wanted to return to England for her confinement. On January 12, 1817, her daughter – and likely Byron's - was born at Bath, a discreet community popular for questionable births. When Allegra was born, Byron was still in Switzerland, missing Augusta and pouring his heart into a drama (or, as he called it, "a dialogue") set in the beautiful Alps that he had so recently climbed.

Allegra

As the fall leaves hailed the start of winter weather, Byron abandoned the Swiss mountains for the warmer climes of Italy, arriving in Venice in November 1816. He wasted no time in seducing his landlord's wife and taking up the study of Armenian at a nearby monastery. It was while there that he was able to read with delight the glowing reviews of the third canto of *Childe Harold* and *The Prisoner of Chillon, and Other Poems*.

In the spring of 1817, Byron journeyed to Rome to join up again with Hobhouse. Continuing his pursuits of all things dark and dreary, he visited the cell where the mad poet Torquato Tasso had been confined during the 16th century, which inspired him to compose *The Lament of Tasso*, one of his darkest works:

> "When the impatient thirst of light and air
>
> Parches the heart; and the abhorred grate,
>
> Marring the sunbeams with its hideous shade,
>
> Works through the throbbing eyeball to the brain
>
> With a hot sense of heaviness and pain;
>
> And bare, at once, Captivity display'd
>
> Stands scoffing through the never-open'd gate,

> Which nothing through its bars admits, save day,
>
> And tasteless food, which I have eat alone
>
> Till its unsocial bitterness is gone;
>
> And I can banquet like a beast of prey,
>
> Sullen and lonely, couching in the cave
>
> Which is my lair, and—it may be—my grave.

Ultimately, he concluded that peace would only come with death:

> "But this is o'er—my pleasant task is done:—
>
> My long-sustaining friend of many years!
>
> If I do blot thy final page with tears,
>
> Know, that my sorrows have wrung from me none.
>
> But thou, my young creation! my soul's child!
>
> Which ever playing round me came and smiled
>
> And woo'd me from myself with that sweet sight,
>
> Thou too art gone—and so is my delight:
>
> And therefore do I weep and inly bleed
>
> With this last bruise upon a broken reed."

Meanwhile, "Manfred" came out on June 16, and it was full of what one critic called its "painful and offensive" theme of incest. While it was indeed a dark poem, the legendary German writer Goethe was among those who praised it. Goethe wrote, "Byron's tragedy, Manfred, was to me a wonderful phenomenon and one that closely touched me. This singular intellectual poet has taken my Faustus to himself and extracted from it the strongest nourishment for his hypochondriac humour. He has made use of the impelling principles in his own way, for his own purposes, so that no one of them remains the same; and it is particularly on this account that I cannot enough admire his genius. The whole is in this way so completely formed anew, that it would be an interesting task for the critic to point out not only the alterations he has made, but their degree of resemblance with, or dissimilarity to, the original; in the course of which I cannot deny that the gloomy heat of an unbounded and exuberant despair becomes at last oppressive to us. Yet is the dissatisfaction we feel always connected with esteem and admiration."

Goethe

While in Rome, Byron began his fourth canto for *Child Harold*, quickly turning out the rough draft but then spending months editing it. However, in the summer of 1817, he found a new interest. Upon hearing a story about a woman whose "dead" husband had returned to her after she had fallen in love with someone else, he became inspired to write a poem based on the experience. He named it "Beppo" and sent it to his publisher on March 25, 1818, with a note that read, "We shall see by this experiment. It will, at any rate, show that I can write cheerfully, and repel the charge of monotony and mannerism." The piece was a success, with the *Monthly Review* asserting that Byron's "satire, though at times a little tinged with vulgarity, is usually good-humoured and often well pointed: he throws about his observations in a lively strain; and it is very amusing to remark how everything, of which he speaks or thinks, becomes the immediate thesis of a new episode of playful moralizing." *Childe Harold, Canto IV*, was also well-received, furthering Byron's reputation.

In July 1818, while living in the large and comfortable Palazzo Mocenigo, Byron wrote to his publisher of two project he had in the works, "one serious & one ludicrous." The latter would become the first canto of his most famous poem, *"Don Juan."* He would work on it for the rest of his life, producing 16 cantos and leaving a 17th unfinished.

A picture of part of the Palazzo Mocenigo

When they saw the first canto, Byron's friends were shocked by the way in which he viciously attacked everyone from the Church to his ex-wife, after whom he obviously modeled Donna Inez, the mother of the title character. Various friends encouraged him to soften some of his language, but he responded to their concerns with typical arrogance, insisting, "The poem will please if it is lively - if it is stupid it will fall - but I will have none of your damned cutting and slashing."

Byron turned 30 in 1818, and the following year he began an affair with Teresa, Contessa Guiccioli, the 19 year old wife of a 54 year old man,. In the four years that followed, the pair would travel together all over Italy. At first, her husband turned a blind eye to it, but in 1820 he demanded a separation. It was for her that Byron wrote "The Prophecy of Dante" in June 1819.

Teresa, Contessa Guiccioli

 The following month, the first two cantos of *Don Juan* were published, causing a backlash unlike any Byron had received before. *Blackwood's Magazine* told readers, "It appears, in short, as if this miserable man, having exhausted every species of sensual gratification, having drained the cup of sin even to its bitterest dregs, were resolved to show us that he is no longer a human being, even in his frailties, but a cool, unconcerned fiend, laughing with a detestable glee over the whole of the better and worse elements of which human life is composed — treating well-nigh with equal derision the most pure of virtues and the most odious of vices, dead alike to the beauty of the one and the deformity of the other — a mere heartless despiser of that frail but noble humanity whose type was never exhibited in a shape of more deplorable degradation than in his own contemptuously distinct delineation of himself."

 Conversely, a few of the more open-minded critics of the day praised the work, with some seeing it as a depiction of the war they believed was raging between nature and civilization. Byron embraced this outlook, writing that *Don Juan* "will be known by and bye for what it is intended a satire on abused of the present states of Society—and not an eulogy of vice."

Inevitably, the scandalous nature of the work helped the cantos sell better, and Byron always claimed that *Don Juan* was semi-autobiographical and that the incidents he described were taken from either his own life of from the lives of other he knew personally.

With no intentions of backing down, Byron continued to work on the poem, beginning the third canto in September 1819 and sending that canto and the fourth canto back to England for publication in February 1820. As he continued that work, he developed an interest in the Carbonari thanks to Teresa's father, Count Ruggero Gamba Ghiselli, and her brother, Count Pietro Gamba. This very secretive group met together regularly to discuss ways in which to overthrow the Austrian government in Italy, and they eventually accepted Byron as one of their own. He in turn purchased arms for them and even allowed them to store their guns and ammunition in his Italian home.

Such underground activities would be enough for most men, but Byron also had his writing, and he even turned his attention to writing plays for private audiences. He composed three such works during his years in Italy. The most autobiographical, *Marino Faliero*, completed in July 1820, tells the story of a 14th century aristocrat who, like Byron, joins forces with the lower classes to fight for freedom. The tale deals with some of Byron's own ambivalence toward the stand he was taking against the members of his own class. He published it a year later, in April 1821, a few months after he released *Don Juan Canto V*. Much to his consternation, it quickly found its way to the public stage.

Even as he continued to work on the next canto for *Don Juan*, Byron remained determined to take shots at the religious beliefs of his day, which he did while writing "Cain, A Mystery." According to one modern author, "Byron has absorbed the ideas of outcast and the wandering Jew, and similar with Augustine, re-elevated Cain to the symbolic representative of witness, which is, without any doubt, not obliged to confirm and testify Christian wholeness...The cursed Jewish wandering in Christian tradition interpreted by Augustine and other theologians is here revised, becoming an alternative 'wandering' guided by Providence, which, in Cain, is not a God-based will, but the human free judgment of morality, as Cain be its witness and protector. When Christian readers reach this very end, they recognize themselves unconsciously as the posterity of this exiling couple by identifying with Byron's revision of Cain and Abel. However, their deep-rooted piety cannot stand such enlightenment. Therefore, there rises the comment that Cain is 'calculated to spread infidelity'...whereas how such infidelity is spread they cannot and dare not clarify, for the divine justice of their God is shattered in this reading experience."

In the meantime, he continued work on *Don Juan*. After seemingly reaching the limits of his own eroticism in the sixth canto, he turned his attention to other aspects of the story, focusing on nobler causes such as war and peace, and men's vain efforts to live with either. Thus, Cantos VII-IX focused on battlefields more than bedrooms. Nonetheless, despite the change in subject matter, John Murray, who had published most of Byron's works, had already had enough and refused to publish more of his "outrageously shocking" volumes.

In 1822, Leigh Hunt, a friend of Mary Shelley's and her husband Percy, joined Percy and Byron in Pisa. The trio had a plan to create a new sort of literary journal that would publish pieces other publications shied away from. Tragically, Percy drowned just days after Hunt arrived, leaving the other two men distraught but determined to go forward with the project, which they named *The Liberal, Verse and Prose From the South*. Through them, Byron met Hunt's brother, John, who agreed to publish the remaining cantos.

Hunt

Percy Shelley

The Funeral of Shelley by Louis Édouard Fournier depicts Hunt and Byron.

In September 1822, Byron and the rest of the group that now called themselves the Pisan Circle left Pisa for Genoa. He was almost finished with *Don Juan Canto X* and began working on the

11th canto, in which he turned his satirical sights on his own people: the English aristocracy. Byron was also looking for a publisher for *The Vision of Judgment*, a satirical version of the popular poem by the same name that Robert Southey had published in April 1821. Byron ultimately contributed *The Vision of Judgment* to the first volume of *The Liberal*, published on October 15, 1822. His work got the publisher, John Hunt, fined for his pains after a court ruled that the piece was a subversive attack on the late King George IV. Today, many consider the piece one of Byron's best.

The Liberal lasted less than a year and put out only four editions, but despite that lack of success and the earlier fine, John Hunt remained Byron's publisher for the rest of the young poet's life. Hunt released Byron's last narratives, including *The Island; or, Christian and His Comrades*, based on the story of the mutiny on the *Bounty*, as well as the *Noble Savage* and *Torquil*, all published in 1823. Though these books were not as popular as some of Byron's earlier works, they still generated respectable sales.

Byron was writing at a furious pace, but he remained restless. In the summer of 1823, Marguerite, Countess of Blessington, recorded an exchange between the two of them: "Byron seems quite decided on going to Greece; yet he talks of this project as if it were more a duty than a pleasure. He asserts that he who is only a poet has done little for mankind, and that he will endeavour to prove in his own person that a poet may be a soldier. That Byron will fulfil this self-imposed duty, is, I think, nearly certain, and that he will fulfil it bravely, I entertain not a doubt…"

With great wisdom and insight into his character, she added, "[F]rom what I have seen of him, I should say that his vocation is more for a reflective than an active life, and that the details and contrarieties to which, from the position he will hold in Greece, he must be subjected, will exhaust his patience and impair his health. If he had only to lead an army to battle, I should have no fear of his acquitting himself well; for the fire and animation of his poetical temperament would carry him thr0ugh such ordeals; notwithstanding the delicacy of his health, which he has greatly impaired by a regime more suited to an ascetic than to a would-be soldier. I can well fancy Byron rushing into the fight, and realizing in the field his poetical ideas of a hero; but I cannot imagine his enduring the tedious details, and submitting to the tiresome discussions and arrangements, of which as a chief he must bear the weight."

Byron did indeed go to Greece to fight in the Greek Revolution against the Ottoman Turks. The Ottomans had been one of the world's great powers since sacking Constantinople in the mid-15th century, but throughout the 19th century and the beginning of the 20th century, the rise of nationalistic aspirations largely contributed to empire's decline. The concept of "nation" was new to the Ottoman Empire, which had thus far thought of subjects as communities built on religion rather than language or geographic origins.

The war of independence in Serbia started in 1804 and would last nearly three decades before the Serbs could declare their freedom. With the facilitation and increasing possibilities of spreading new ideas, the Christian Serbs asked themselves why they still lived in serfdom under Muslim rule while Christians just across the border enjoyed freedom and self-governance. The Serbian intellectuals gathered inspiration and knowledge from both the Austrian Empire and the Russian Empire.

One of the strongest identities maintained through the Orthodox Church was a powerful elite group known as the *Phanariotes*, a Greek one. The existing Greek nationalistic sentiment had already been stirred by Russia, which saw the Greeks as allies in the struggle against the Ottomans. The new Russian intelligentsia saw their emerging empire as the successor of the Byzantine Empire. This heritage was underlined by Russia's coat of arms, the double-headed eagle, formerly associated with Constantinople and the Eastern Roman Empire. On the political level, this narrative was seen as a way to influence the various peoples under Ottoman rule in the Balkans by attracting those who sought independence. It was no coincidence that Alexander Ypsilantis, a central figure of the Greek independence movement, served in the Russian army. However, the context of the uprising that broke out in 1821 made it different from previous revolts sponsored by Russia.

Ypsilantis

The aspirations of the peoples ruled by the Ottomans were fueled by the ideas of the French Revolution in 1789. The revolution saw the emergence of the concept of "patrie" (Fatherland) and pitted the "patriotes" against the old nobility. The Greeks were particularly influenced by new ideas coming from Western Europe. Greek merchants travelled through Europe while elements among the Greek elite, the Phanariotes, cultivated their difference and supported the diffusion of such ideas by financing schools and books promoting it. This growth of the Greek national culture and sentiment, known as the Modern Greek Enlightenment, resulted in the sentiment among Greeks that they were part of one separate nation. In 1814, in the Russian city of Odessa,[1] these ideas led to the creation of a new secret society, the *Filiki Eteria* or Society of Friends, aimed at ending the Ottoman rule over Greece. The society attracted many members of the Greek diaspora. This included Ypsilantis, who became the head of the society on July 15, 1820, after the then Russian Foreign Minister and Ionian-born Ioannis Antonios Kapodistrias refused it.

On his way to Greece, Byron carried with him as much money and medical supplies as he could, as well as the elaborate uniforms and helmets he had commissioned to wear during his endeavors. It's somewhat telling that he left England still undecided about which side he would fight on, but given the political context of the brewing revolution and his past travels in Greece, it is no surprise that he ultimately chose to fight with the rebels. In November 1823, he loaned some of the Greek leaders 4,000 pounds with which to purchase a naval fleet, and in January 1824, he donned his bright red uniform and joined Prince Alexander Mavrokordatos in Missolonghi to discuss more plans for their enterprise.

---

[1] Present day Ukraine.

The reception of Lord Byron at Missolonghi by **Theodoros Vryzakis**

Later that month, as his birthday approached, he wrote the tragically prophetic "On this Day I Complete my Thirty-Sixth Year."

>'Tis time this heart should be unmoved,
>
>>Since others it hath ceased to move:
>
>Yet though I cannot be beloved,
>
>>Still let me love!

>My days are in the yellow leaf;
>
>>The flowers and fruits of Love are gone;
>
>The worm—the canker, and the grief
>
>>Are mine alone!

The fire that on my bosom preys

    Is lone as some Volcanic Isle;

No torch is kindled at its blaze

        A funeral pile.

The hope, the fear, the jealous care,

    The exalted portion of the pain

And power of Love I cannot share,

        But wear the chain.

But 'tis not thus—and 'tis not here

    Such thoughts should shake my Soul, nor now,

Where Glory decks the hero's bier,

        Or binds his brow.

The Sword, the Banner, and the Field,

    Glory and Greece around us see!

The Spartan borne upon his shield

        Was not more free.

Awake (not Greece—she is awake!)

    Awake, my Spirit! Think through whom

>
> Thy life-blood tracks its parent lake
>
> And then strike home!
>
> Tread those reviving passions down
>
> Unworthy Manhood—unto thee
>
> Indifferent should the smile or frown
>
> Of beauty be.
>
> If thou regret'st thy Youth, why live?
>
> The land of honourable Death
>
> Is here:—up to the Field, and give
>
> Away thy breath!
>
> Seek out—less often sought than found—
>
> A Soldier's Grave, for thee the best;
>
> Then look around, and choose thy Ground,
>
> And take thy rest.

It would be among his last works, because in the months that followed, all the mistakes of his life seemed to catch up with him at once.

The 15th and 16th Cantos of *Don Juan* were panned by critics, with the *Literary Gazette* was particularly scathing: "Lord Byron's name is not affixed to this continuation of *Don Juan* ; and it is so destitute of the least glimmering of talent, so wretched a piece of stuff altogether, that we are inclined to believe it the work of some imitator, inferior in his best efforts to even the worst of the genuine bad Cantos which have preceded. If it be really Lord Byron's, it is a sad proof of his very mistaken opinion, that whatever nonsense he may think proper to scribble is worthy of being read. But we cannot believe it to be his;-it must be an attempt to gull the public by some worthy brother…"

Byron, having spent his short life involving himself in all types of scandals and debauchery, was also beginning to pay the price physically. In April 1824, he went out riding on a stormy day without the proper protective gear and returned home soaked to the bone. He subsequently came down with a bad cold that soon evolved into some sort of rheumatic issue. His doctors wanted to bleed him to treat the fever and other maladies, a suggestion he wisely ignored in the beginning. However, as his condition worsened, he gave into them and subjected himself to several bleedings, which further weakened him. On the evening of Monday, April 19, 1824, as a storm raged outside his window, Byron slipped away. He was just 36 years old.

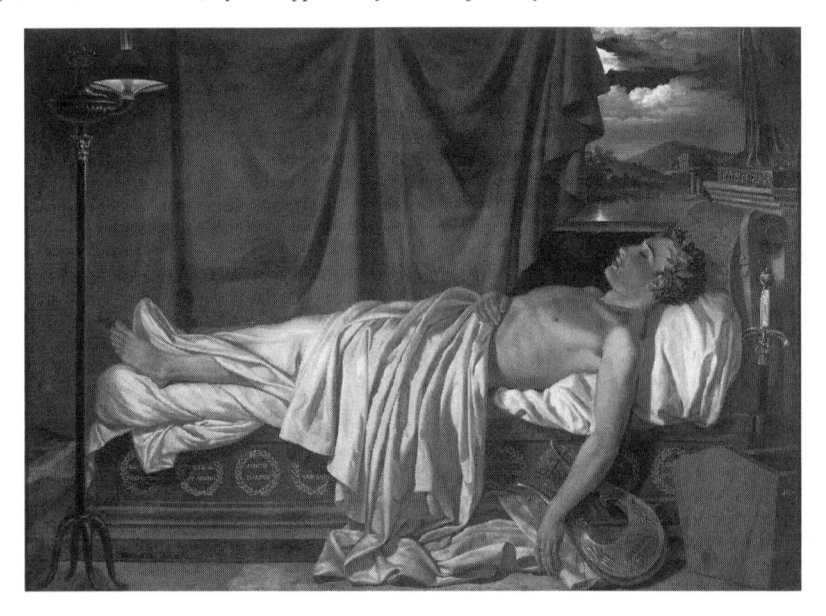

Lord Byron on His Deathbed by Joseph Denis Odevaere (circa 1826)

In the end, of course, Byron was sure to live on through his work, but it was unclear exactly what his legacy would be. In 1831, Thomas Babington Macaulay wrote in the *Edinburgh Review*, "During the twenty years which followed the death of Cowper, the revolution in English poetry was fully consummated. None of the writers of this period…contributed so much to the consummation as Lord Byron." At the same time, he noted, "Yet he, Lord Byron, contributed to it unwillingly, and with constant self-reproach and shame. All his tastes and inclinations led him to take part with the school of poetry which was going out, against the school which was coming in." In a letter to relatives that same year, Macaulay was even more blunt, writing, "I never heard a single expression of fondness for him fall from the lips of any of those who knew him well."

As Macaulay's words indicate, Byron's contemporaries understood his artistic abilities, but they were shocked at the manner in which he flagrantly violated the social mores of the day. As a result, even while Byron was being immortalized as a hero in Greece because of his participation in their fight for independence, to the extent that the anniversary of his death is commemorated by the Greeks as "Byron Day," it would take several generations for one of the most famous writers of all time to receive the proper recognition back home. While so many of Britain's most famous writers were buried at Westminster Abbey, Lord Byron's grave is located at St Mary Magdalene, in Hucknall, Notts, where he rests alongside Ada, the daughter he never really knew. It would not be until 1969 that Westminster Abbey finally relented and accepted a memorial in tribute to him.

A statue of Lord Byron in Athens

Online Resources

Other books about poetry by Charles River Editors

Other books about Lord Byron on Amazon

Further Reading

Garrett, Martin: George Gordon, Lord Byron. (British Library Writers' Lives). London: British Library, 2000.

Garrett, Martin. Palgrave Literary Dictionary of Byron. Palgrave, 2010.

Guiccioli, Teresa, contessa di, Lord Byron's Life in Italy, transl. Michael Rees, ed. Peter Cochran, 2005.

Grosskurth, Phyllis: Byron: The Flawed Angel. Hodder, 1997.

Free Books by Charles River Editors

We have brand new titles available for free most days of the week. To see which of our titles are currently free, click on this link.

Discounted Books by Charles River Editors

We have titles at a discount price of just 99 cents everyday. To see which of our titles are currently 99 cents, click on this link.

Printed in Great Britain
by Amazon